Thoughts On Fire:

A Collection of Poems From The Road of Life

Craig Collette

Copyright © 2014 Craig Collette

All rights reserved. No part of this book may be reproduced, stored in a retrieval system, or transmitted by any means without the prior written permission of the publisher.

Morning Light Publishers: **morninglightpublishers@aol.com**

ISBN: 0615933556

ISBN-13: 978-0615933559

DEDICATION

This labor of love is respectfully dedicated to the memory of my two grandfathers: Will Collette and Anatole Serrette, Sr. They were both story tellers extraordinaire and it is from hearing their stories over and over as a child that I get this great love for telling my own stories through poetry. Long live the memories.

TABLE OF CONTENTS

Acknowledgements	ix
Death of The Old Eskimo	1
Drinker of The Wind	2-3
A Million Stars	4
Touch My Soul	5
The Madness Which Is	5
Don't Rake The Leaves	6
The Wine of Evermore	7
Father Time and His Great Horn	8-10
And I Miss You	11
The Ancient Samurai	12-13
Frosty December Dusk	14-15
I Am Bayou	15-17
Moonstruck	17
Leave A Man Alone With His Thoughts	18-19
Ungathered Roses	19-20
Tampering With Fate	21
You Will Never Be Forgotten	22-23
Feelings	24

TABLE OF CONTENTS

Dead Dreams Broken	25-26
Blue Men of The Sahara	27-28
Rose Lip Maidens	28
Deep Dark Space	29
Autumn	29
A Day In Jerusalem	30-31
Ashes And Albatrosses	31
Some Things	32
Silence	32
Free Thinking	32
The Thistle Song	33
The Abandoned Garden	34-36
The Dragonfly	36
Achilles And The Mirror	37
Born In The Swamp	38-39
Pride	39
Purple Cotton	40-41
Crooked Hands	41
Thoughts On Fire	42-44

ACKNOWLEDGEMENTS

Just as it can be said that no book ever writes itself and that no author is an island unto himself, so I have been greatly helped by several people as I have worked to bring this labor of love to fruition.

First, is R.E. Clark, an author, publisher, minister and friend. He provided valuable insight at just the right times. Without his gracious input it's hard to imagine how much longer this book might have remained unpublished.

Second, is Cassie LeJeune, who although very busy as a wife, mother and teacher, was kind enough to edit this work during her precious spare time. Her editing skills and keen eye for detail cannot be overstated. If there are mistakes they are mine, not hers.

Finally, my oldest daughter, Jane C. Heels, provided the back cover photo. Although very busy herself as a wife, homemaker and Ph.D. student, she also loves to take pictures and provided the perfect photo.

If this work is deemed to be a success, then they deserve credit for helping to make it so. I am ever grateful to them for their help.

Death of The Old Eskimo

Put me out on the ice to die. Let the snow fall all around me,

And on me until at last I become a real snowman.

Let the winds of Thor howl, and the seal and the walrus cry.

Let the great white bear come and carry my soul away.

I have fulfilled my destiny and my purpose and lived the way of my fathers.

Never again will my spear pierce flesh, or my lips taste blood and blubber.

Let another have my igloo; I no longer need its warmth and comfort.

My woman is gone, I'm not even half of a man; I have outlived both valor and desire.

May my sled carry my children's children and the memory of me live on forever.

I'll miss those that I've loved and nourished; I'll miss the feel of the cold sea on my face.

Alas, I go the way of all flesh. I go to the great igloo of my forefathers,

But I give myself freely to the cold and die with a frozen teardrop upon my cheek.

Drinker of The Wind

You drink up the wind like fire

Racing across the hot desert sands,

Head held high in your proud, Arabian style,

Living up to all the great Bedouins' demands.

Tails carried high, nostrils all aflare,

Drawing speed, strength and courage from the wind;

And with the trumpet sound of Mohammed calling,

You would ever prove your loyalty in the end.

Thunder and lightning on four strong legs,

Extraordinarily graceful, floating above the ground.

Snorting and neighing, mane flying in the wind,

Father of the best horses ever found.

Legend has it that your creation was divine:

A wind sprout swirling across the hot desert floor

Gathered itself together into a fine, prancing horse.

And so you were cast into legend forevermore.

With divine blood coursing through your veins,
It's no wonder that you could fly like the wind.
Eyes of fire, and the angel Gibril upon your back,
You were great, there was no need to pretend.

Bred for fighting, sparks flying from your hooves,
Standing steady against both arrow and spear.
Unafraid of the blood and gore of war,
You would plunge into battle without fear.

You could outrun the striped zebra and swift gazelle,
So your good masters were always well fed.
You were the honor of many a sultan and sheikh
And often to their fine stables were led.

You've been the desire of every Arabian
And the possession of many others as well:
Solomon, Napoleon, royalty of England and France;
Still the stuff of which legends will ever tell.

So into the 21st century your legend thrives,
The horse to which all other horses aspire.
You were great when blown into existence
And your greatness passes on from sire to sire.

A Million Stars

A million stars flutter in the night sky,
Painting the universe with dazzling colors of light.
Splattered across heaven like broken pieces of a rainbow,
All of darkness, all so bright.

Suspended like celestial fixtures arrayed in grand design,
Shadowless ornaments emanating bright and clear.
Standing guard over the dark secrets of space and time,
Ever far away, ever so near.

Silently singing that all creation might hear,
A somber chorus of music unrestrained,
Telling of God's splendor in all that He has made,
Proclaiming His glory with lips unstained.

A million stars flutter in the night sky
Like flames igniting the imagination;
Like mythical characters caught up in a cosmic drama,
Captivating audiences from generation to generation.

Touch My Soul

Move gingerly now

As the feathers of

Your warm breath

Touch my face,

Touch my soul.

The Madness Which Is

A blood-stained

White rose

And my heart

Still warm

In my trembling hands.

All around

Dreams are shattered

Like glass,

Strewn about

By the madness

Which is.

Don't Rake The Leaves

Don't rake the leaves.

Don't cut them or blow them.

Don't light that sacred fall fire yet;

Let them linger a bit longer.

Let the wind play with them a bit more,

Teasing them as the sun lights up the world.

Give the yard just one more day

To enjoy their peaceful,

Scattered presence,

Their multicolored glory.

Give the golds

And reds

And yellows

Just a bit more time

To color my world,

To light up my life.

Let me enjoy their un-raked,

Un-cut,

Un-blown,

And un-burnt beauty.

Let my soul savor their rich contribution

To a sometimes ugly world.

The Wine Of Evermore

Come,

Let us fill our cups

With the sweet wine of life

While we still have breath,

And still have eyes

To behold life's beauty.

For who knows that tomorrow

Our cups may be wrenched

From our feeble hands,

And darkness on our eyes descends,

Our breath fleeting like the wind.

And those among us

Who have to Christ fled in life

Will to Him flee in death,

Our feeble hands restored,

Grasping again our joyful cups,

Now filled with heavens' wine,

That we may enjoy its glories

Evermore.

Father Time And His Great Horn

I dreamed as I lay sleeping

That I saw Father Time.

He stood upon the rim of the void

Casting a pale, endless shadow.

His beard was long and gray,

As you might expect of one so old.

His eyes were peaceful and wise,

His countenance, solemn but dreadful.

As he stood silhouetted against the universe,

He raised a great horn to his lips

And blew out a piercing sound

Which was at once both beautiful and terrible.

As the sound slowly traveled,

Everything trembled in its wake,

The very foundations of the universe shook in awe.

The innumerable stars all paid homage.

After what seemed like forever,

A light could be seen racing through the cosmos.

Even as it came worlds dissolved into flames,

Darkness itself fled before it in haste.

And there stood Father Time with an outstretched arm,

In his well worn hand, a clear, unsealed jar.

Then came the light and the darkness and the flames,

Indeed, everything which ever was, and poured themselves into the jar.

Having resealed the jar containing all that ever was,

He now stood alone in the void.

No one knows how long, for no one even existed.

But there he stood, jar and horn in hand.

Then after a second or an eternity (no one knows),

He again blew his great horn and began to shake the jar.

As he did, lightning flashed and thunder peeled

Within the jar, and something strange began to happen:

Little by little the jar began to shrink,

Even as the lightning grew more and more intense.

Then he raised the jar high above his aged head

And blew out one final note on his great horn.

As soon as that final note sounded,

The jar shrank to nothing and exploded,

And out burst countless points of light

Scattering madly like leaves before a storm.

Each point of light, like shattered fragments of a rainbow,

Hastened to its appointed destination and purpose:

Becoming new worlds, all life and all that would ever be,

Leaving Father Time and his great horn behind.

Still he stood alone, but now in the newness of it all:

New worlds remade from the dust and ashes of the old,

New life remade from the hopes and dreams of the old,

New light, new darkness, new flames to burn brighter than the old.

Then majestically he lay down and slept.

His work done, he sought to be undisturbed.

And as the mists of time clouded my mind,

I drifted out of my dreams, and he into his.

And I Miss You

Feels like I've been

On the dark side of the moon.

I feel so far away,

Like words without a tune.

Feels like I've been

Looking up from the ocean floor;

Down where it's dark and cold

And I can hide from the savage bore.

And I miss you.

Feels like you've been

Gone for a million years;

Like time has never been

And I'm frozen in my tears.

Feels like the world

Is a place that's hard to be,

'Cause living without you

Has taken its toll on me.

The Ancient Samurai

I hear the sound,

The quiet whisper

Of the ancient Samurai

As his sword is unsheathed.

The sound of steel on leather,

The sound of death

On the battle field of life.

The fast,

Well bred horse

Does not shy from the task at hand

As he flies like a fiend,

Fiercely neighing and snorting,

Gore dripping around him like honey

And blood pouring out like wine.

On his back,

The Samurai:

Great warrior and wise.

Ever the friend of Japan

And the old and honorable ways.

I see them now,

Horse and rider,

Grace under pressure

As blades crash like thunder

And strike like lightning.

But all things must come to an end

As the great wheel of time

Rolls on.

And so horse and rider

Ride off into the pages of history,

Bearing away an ancient custom:

A way of life for so many.

But if you listen long,

Bending your ear to the wind,

You can still hear the sound

Of the Samurai sword,

Of the hoof beats of great steeds,

And the quiet whisper

Of the ancient Samurai himself.

Frosty December Dusk

In the frosty December dusk,

Canadian geese calling out overhead,

We stood outdoors and felt the chill

Knowing that winter had indeed arrived.

Our summer clothes had long been put up,

Neatly packed away into many a bag and box.

Until then we had yet to don our winter's best.

But alas, this day's end was a harbinger of change.

The wood pile would get good use now,

Neglected as it had been up to this point.

The remaining leaves would soon surely die,

Even as winter flowers were coming to life.

Walking in the woods would be different too,

Now that the mosquitoes would finally be gone.

It's much easier to put on more clothes

Than to constantly fight those pesky things.

Ducks would be coming down in earnest as well,

As would other birds heading south for the winter.

The north's loss is always our gain this time of year,

So we heartily welcome this frosty December dusk.

I Am Bayou

I am bayou,

I've been in Louisiana

A long, long time.

I'm not sure how old I am,

But I was here the last time

That the mighty Mississippi changed course.

I'm known by many different names:

Teche, Vermillion, D'arbonne,

Manchac, Nez-Picque, Chene.

I was a friend to the Indians,

Their mystical and moss draped highway.

The Cajuns knew me romantically,

Evangeline herself did ply my waters

In search of her long lost love, Gabriel.

Many dug outs, pirogues,

Skiffs and boats of all kinds

Have plied my waters as well,

My wet fingers stretching all across the bayou state.

Countless battles have been fought on my waves and banks

As I wind strategically through

Swamps and prairies and towns and bottoms,

My own muddy bottom a watery grave for too many.

I feed off rivers and lakes

From the Gulf of Mexico to Spring Hill,

From Bogalousa to Lockport.

Fish too numerous to name call me home,

As do people from around the world,

Living in lavish mansions

And on simple houseboats.

I'm friendly when the fish are biting,

The source of a nice day out,

But treacherous and deadly

When my flood waters rise,

The horror of a drowning

Or a flooded home.

I've been spoken to

In many different languages:

French, Italian, German,

English, Spanish,

Not to mention a host of Indian tongues.

I remember steamboats.

I remember cypress log jams.

I remember plantations and slaves,

Cotton gins and sugar cane mills.

My memory is rich and deep.

I treasure who I am:

I am bayou,

I've been in Louisiana

A long, long time.

Moonstruck

Midnight's soft

Sweet hush

Came quietly,

Like a blush,

And found me

Struck by the moon.

Leave A Man Alone With His Thoughts

Leave a man alone

With his thoughts,

Leave them undisturbed.

For without knowing it,

You might upset one of his

Greatest moments.

He may never

Win that race,

Write that song,

Reach that star,

Or discover love's mystery.

You just never know.

A man and his thoughts

Are precious these days

In a world which is so noisy

And so much of our thinking

Is done for us.

Don't disturb that man

Staring out into the dark of night,

Eyes glazed over

And fixed on eternity.

Paralyzed by the stars,

He's rendered temporarily useless

To all but himself.

Involuntarily suspended

In space and time,

He's in a place

That's his and his alone,

So

Leave a man alone

With his thoughts.

Ungathered Roses

Ungathered roses

Neither cut nor draw blood.

How can they?

We fear to touch them,

Yet they are so pure.

Were I but the wind,

Or perhaps a passing thought,

I might brush up against one

As it remained unspoiled upon the branch;

And not having been cut,

Nor spilt blood,

I might rejoice at my good fortune.

But alas,

Even to touch a thing of beauty

Is not to hold it in your hand.

We must brave the thorns,

Risking the cuts

And the blood

If we are to truly appreciate

Each petal,

Indeed the whole,

For all it's worth.

We must gather

The ungathered roses

While there is still time,

While we still have the courage,

While they are still alive

And while there yet remain

Ungathered roses.

Tampering With Fate

I'd like to try my hand

Now and again,

But fear tampering with

The dark machinery of fate.

Drawn in the sand,

It's a fine line

Which we tread,

The outcome to await.

I'd buy the moon

Just to own it,

Then swallow the sun

As it slowly burns,

But none are immune

From human suffering

And it's sure that time

Never, ever returns.

You Will Never Be Forgotten

Your blood has been spilt,

Your bones shattered

By people who under different circumstances

Might well have been your friends.

You will never be forgotten.

You sailed the world over,

Tasting the salty sea air

Of a thousand deadly battles

In seas whose names you couldn't pronounce.

You will never be forgotten.

You stormed hell bent beaches,

Lived and died in blood stained trenches,

Fighting for something greater than yourselves:

The freedom of others.

You will never be forgotten.

You came from big cities and small towns

All across our great nation,

Leaving behind family and friends,

Farms and sky scrapers, hopes and dreams.

You will never be forgotten.

Yours was the luck of the damned
As you fought in the jungles, in the mountains,
In small villages, on big ships
And in planes you always dreamed of flying.
You will never be forgotten.

You fought bravely and died nobly,
Fighting tyrants and despots and
Madmen trying to rule the world.
You sacrificed for a freedom dearly cherished.
Thank you, you will never be forgotten.

Feelings

I felt the brush

Of your breath

Upon my cheek,

And heard the sounds

Of a thousand

Morning trains

As the stars fled

From the

Rosy fingers

Of dawn.

I felt the touch

Of your hand

Upon my chest,

And heard the sounds

Which only

Lovers make

As the night

Fled quietly

And

Was gone.

Dead Dreams Broken

Dead

Dreams

Broken

Words

Unspoken

Silent wings

Flutter

Above

Dry springs

While we

Thirst

And

Songs

Remain unsung

And

Promises

Un-kept fall

On

Deaf ears

With

Darkness glistening

Listening

Quietly

To

Dead men

With

Such

Cold warmth

And

Eyes unseeing

And

Hearts

Fleeing

Life's pain

On a

Dark train

Of

Unclaimed

Forgotten memories

And

Dead

Dreams

Broken

Blue Men of The Sahara

The young camel wanders after its mother

In a desert which is both intriguing and mysterious.

The winds are as hot and as fierce as the sun,

Which is both a source of life and of death for all.

There's little pasture for the cow and the goat;

Ours is an endless sea of sand and wind-blown dunes.

Shadows are long and the nights even longer,

As we sit around our fires linking the present to the past.

We are the princes of the desert: the Tuareg.

Ours has been a long, hard and often bitter story,

As we have been nomads in a no-man's land,

Since before the time of our fathers' fathers.

We have lived by both the sword and the gun;

It has been a way of life in our sun-soaked land,

Where the jackal runs with the camel,

And the gray hawk is master of the skies.

Some have called us "the blue men of the Sahara."

We are a proud and noble race.

Our swords are sacred and passed on for generations;

They carry the spirit and power of ancient nomads.

We have been traders for thousands of years,

Crossing the Sahara in endless camel caravans

With goods from the south, bound for the world,

Guided by the sun, the stars and our knowledge of the desert.

Give us our tents, our camels and our songs;

Give us our wives, our children and our way of life.

We don't ask for much but will kill and die

For what is ours if you leave us no other choice.

Rose Lip Maidens

Rose lip maidens,

Light foot lads,

These turn into mothers,

The others into dads.

Deep Dark Space

I saw your face

Like a familiar ghost

In a dream,

And all my

Thoughts shattered

Like a hammer

On glass;

Like a supernova exploding

In deep, dark space.

Autumn

Autumn,

That time of year

When we go outdoors

And soak up the changing seasons.

Gorgeous.

A Day In Jerusalem

I stepped back through time,
Through corridors hallowed and divine,
Through centuries and layers of archaeology,
And life and death and devotion.
I was in Jerusalem.

I wandered trance-like down the Via Dolorosa,
Stopping at the different stations of the cross,
Thinking back on all that it meant then
And all that it means these centuries later.
I was at Golgotha.

I was surrounded by masses of people,
Yet often found myself eerily alone,
Walking through places which
Awakened every sense possibly known to man.
I was in the old market.

I thought that I heard ancient voices
Wafting mysteriously on a gentle wind:
Prayers uttered in a thousand different tongues
Violently beseeching heaven itself.
I was at the Wailing Wall.

My feet stood where prophets had tread
And felt the struggle of countless generations.
Looking down from above the holy city
In all of its beauty and vulgarity.
I was on the Mount of Olives.

Ashes and Albatrosses

I was an albatross

                                    Last night in a dream,

             Flying through the mirrors

                                    In my mind.

      I was the king

                 Of a kingdom of ashes,

                              Flying through the clouds

         In my head.

So far away,   so very far away.

Some Things

Some things

Never escape the mind,

That prison

With velvet chains.

Silence

Lying all alone,

The silence is deafening

And keeps me awake.

Free Thinking

I sat there

Quietly lost in thought,

Enjoying for free

What could never be bought.

The Thistle Song

Morning clung to the thistles

Like dew to the grass

After night had spoken

All that it could say

To the darkness.

And who knows

What was said?

A hush to tremble

Fell on the slumbering world

As the morning fair

Fought to free itself

From bitter watches

Of the night,

The lingering night.

And as the sun fell free

From nights' dark clutch,

The thistles sang

A song of renewed hope;

Dripping dew like honey

After pale springs have melted

And winter's plague was broken.

The Abandoned Garden

Wandering through

An abandoned garden

And feeling the absence

Of what once was,

Like the bitter sting

Of winter

On the face

Of life.

Lost,

We gingerly step

On dead leaves

Now decaying

As death's eerie shadow,

New to this place,

Shrouds us in

Its unnatural

And ungodly

Darkness.

This paradise lost,

Once so full

Of life

And all things good,

Has now become

A wasteland

Of sins' dark deeds.

The innocence

And nakedness

Have turned to shame,

And Gods' voice,

Once so pleasant,

And a thing

To be desired,

Has turned into

The soul's

Darkest terror,

And a sound

From which

To hide.

Truth

Has been traded

For a lie,

And the mosaic

Of life colors

Has faded to

Black and white.

But all is not

Without hope;

The Master has

His plan

And it

Will not be

Thwarted.

He who owns

All time

And every garden

Is about His work

As He sees fit.

The curse

Will be undone

And

The abandoned garden

Restored.

The Dragonfly

The dragonfly tried

Time and again to get in.

Glass---now his head hurts.

Achilles And The Mirror

Ever the fires of hell

Nip at our heels,

And Achilles,

Oh Achilles,

Great warrior but weak,

Where are you now?

Where treads your wounded heel?

Where now the strength

Once yours

As you plowed men

And the powers of hell

Into the ground

Like harrows

Into thrice plowed soil?

Where now Achilles,

Altered ego,

Now that

The mirror has shattered

And the shards and blood

Lie mercilessly

At your once faithful feet,

Ever the reminders

Of the endless war

For your soul.

Born In The Swamp

I was born in the swamp.

My father was a 12' gator;

My mother, a lovely night heron.

My brothers were blue crawfish;

My sisters, adorable water lilies.

Dark waters course through my veins;

Spanish moss grows for hair.

I speak the language of the turtles

And dance upon the water.

The shadows are my food;

The gentle breeze is what I drink.

Crickets and frogs make the music here

While leaves are the song masters.

My grandfathers were tall cypress trees,

Their knees poking out of the murky waters.

My grandmothers were the sounds that you heard

And the lightning which you saw in thunderstorms.

I played with the nutria as a child

And swam with the catfish and choupique.

I ran through the woods with the deer

And chased black squirrels up cottonwood trees.

I was born in the swamp.

My name is written in mud.

My people have long been here;

Their voices echo in the night,

Their memories write our history.

Pride

Pride is the death

Of many

Hopes and dreams

As it thunders

Recklessly

Like Zeus,

Drunk on

The blood

Of

His enemies.

Purple Cotton

The white cotton tops look purple

In the lazy afternoon shadows

As we pass multiple small cotton fields,

None more than four acres in size.

"I didn't realize that cotton

Grew this far north," I said,

Topping another hill on Hwy. 49

Between Asheboro and Charlotte, N.C.

I could easily get addicted to this,

Even if I don't have a spinning wheel,

And haven't picked cotton for 45 years.

This is a beautiful stretch of highway.

A speeding car does absolutely

No justice to a moment such as this.

One needs to get out and touch

The cotton with his very soul,

To stop and smell the cotton.

And taking a stem in his hands,

Pull the "purple" white puff apart

'Til at last it seems like cotton candy

In the hands of an awestruck child.

Ah, life is such a vapor in the wind,

A bubble in the mountain stream.

But cotton, purple cotton, never dies.

It lives on forever in fertile soils

And in fertile imaginations

As the lazy afternoon shadows of life

Get plowed into the coming night.

Crooked Hands

I built an empire of dirt

With my own crooked hands;

Taking what was not mine,

Only to realize

That I had

Stolen from myself.

Thoughts On Fire

Words

Spring out

From

Who knows

Where

Like a tiger

With a

Wild look

In his eyes

Lashing his tail

Then

Springing out

Of the shadows

Like a bolt

Of lightning

So

The writer

Lashes

His pen

And

Splashes

And

Slashes

His pages

Until

At last

His soul

Is emptied

Of its

Mysterious

Burden

Yet

Unconsumed

By the

Flames

He returns

Again and

Again

To the

Page

For he

Is compelled

By

Something

Greater than

Himself

Something

Greater than

His ability

To stop

That which

Cannot

Be stopped

For ever

The flame

Burns

And

Ever he

Lives

With his

Thoughts

On

Fire

www.ingramcontent.com/pod-product-compliance
Lightning Source LLC
Chambersburg PA
CBHW061259040426
42444CB00010B/2433